Totem Pole

Jennifer Howse

Weigl

Published by Weigl Educational Publishers Limited
6325 10th Street SE
Calgary, Alberta T2H 2Z9
Website: www.weigl.com

Library and Archives Canada Cataloguing in Publication

Howse, Jennifer
          Totem poles : Canadian icons / Jennifer Howse.
Includes index.
Also available in electronic format.
ISBN 978-1-77071-574-5 (bound).--ISBN 978-1-77071-581-3 (pbk.)
          1. Totem poles--Canada--Juvenile literature. 2. Indian
sculpture--Canada--Juvenile literature. I. Title.

E98.T65H69 2010   j730'.8997071   C2010-903739-1

Printed in the United States of America in North Mankato, Minnesota
1 2 3 4 5 6 7 8 9 0 14 13 12 11 10

072010
WEP230610

Editor: Heather Kissock
Design: Terry Paulhus

Weigl acknowledges Getty Images and Alamy as image suppliers for this title.

Every reasonable effort has been made to trace ownership and to obtain permission to reprint copyright material.
The publishers would be pleased to have any errors or omissions brought to their attention so that they may be
corrected in subsequent printings.

We acknowledge the financial support of the Government of Canada through the Canada Book Fund for our
publishing activities.

CONTENTS

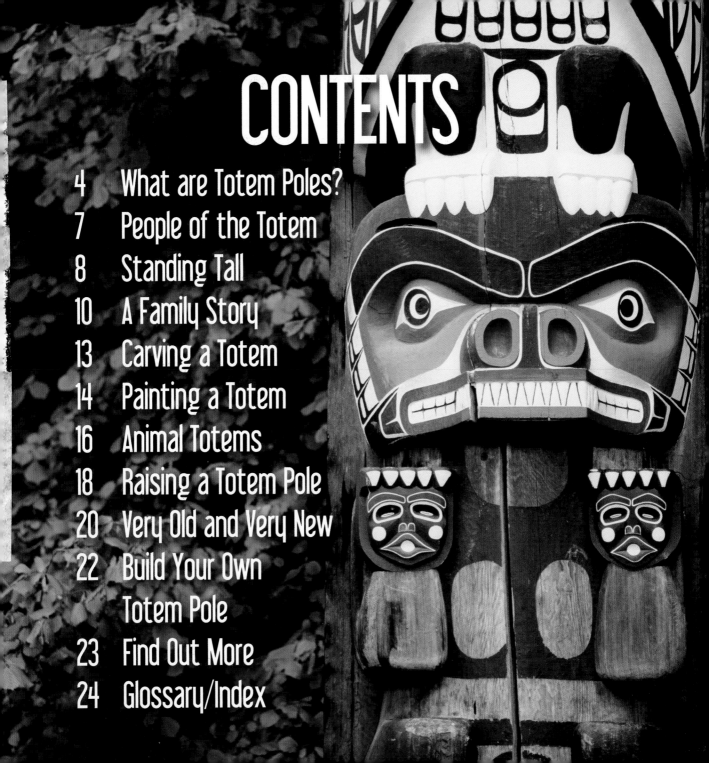

What are Totem Poles?

A totem pole is a tall wooden carving made from a tree trunk. It has shapes of animals and other creatures stacked on top of each other. Totems, or figures, often honour a family's **ancestors** or **First Nations heritage**. Totem poles are found throughout western British Columbia. They are an important **cultural symbol** for the First Nations of the northwest coast.

People of the Totem

Making totem poles is a long-held **tradition** for many First Nations living along the Pacific Northwest. Totem poles have different meanings for each First Nation. They can also have many uses. Totem poles can be family memorials, grave posts, house posts, doorway poles, and welcome poles.

Standing Tall

Totem poles can be seen in many places, including parks, museums, and villages. They are found along the coast of British Columbia and as far north as Alaska. They can be seen as far south as Washington state.

Often, totem poles face the ocean or a river. They have been placed there to welcome visitors.

A Family Story

People who carve totem poles are important members of their community. Carvers help families plan and make their totem poles. First, the family chooses the figures they want on the pole. Then, the family decides where each figure will be placed on the pole. The carver creates the design and decides how each figure will look.

Carving a Totem

Carving a totem is hard work that takes a long time. First, the carver **fells** a tree. Most often, the tree is a tall red cedar. The tree log is brought to the village and laid down. The carver strips the sap and bark from the log. Then, the carver uses charcoal to draw the plan of the totem onto the log.

A carver needs sharp carving knives. A large **adze** is used to remove big pieces of wood from the log. A smaller adze is used to create the detail of the design.

Painting a Totem

Once a totem pole is carved, it is painted. Some paint is made by grinding a **mineral** into a fine powder. The powder is mixed with oil from salmon eggs. Paint colors include black, red, yellow, blue, green, and white. The bright colours bring the totems to life.

In the past, paintbrushes were made from porcupine hair. The hair was attached to a cedar wood handle.

15

Animal Totems

Most totem poles have figures of animals. Some of the animals include the beaver, bear, eagle, and raven. Animals from the ocean are also shown. These may include the whale and shark.

Each animal represents different qualities. Bumblebees are a symbol of honesty. Bears represent strength. Doves show love. The animals chosen to be on a family's totem pole have great meaning to the family.

Raising a Totem Pole

The people of the community come together to carry the pole to the place where it will stand. Then, the pole is placed in a hole. Ropes, poles, and hard work are used to pull the pole upright. The figures on the totem pole are explained to the community. This helps everyone understand the importance of the pole.

Often, there is a **potlatch** in honour of the new totem pole. People join in singing, drumming, and dancing.

Very Old and Very New

In the past, totem poles were short. Some were only as tall as a ski pole. Totem poles became larger and more detailed after First Nations began trading with Europeans. Europeans brought new metal carving tools to the First Nations. This helped carvers make the taller totem poles of today.

Very old totem poles can be found in the village of Kitwancool, in British Columbia. One of the tallest totem poles is found in the village of Alert Bay. It is made from three logs joined together.

Build Your Own Totem Pole

Supplies

pen

paper

popsicle sticks

paintbrush

modelling clay or other
soft modelling material

paint

1. Think of four figures that you like. They can be animals, such as a cat or dog. The figures can also be people you feel are important.

2. Using the figures you have chosen, sketch your totem pole on a piece of paper.

3. Mould the clay material into the shape of a log.

4. Lay the clay log on its side, and carve your four figures into it. Use your sketch as your model.

5. Paint the figures to add colour.

6. After the paint has dried, raise your totem pole, and stand it upright.

7. Show your friends and family your totem pole. Explain what each figure means to you and why you have chosen it.

Find Out More

To find out more about totem poles and the people of the Pacific Northwest Coast, visit these websites.

Carving at Skidegate
www.spruceroots.org/
PoleSite/Haida.html

How Stuff Works
http://people.
howstuffworks.com/
totem-pole.htm

TotemPole.net
www.totem-pole.net

Simon Fraser Museum of Archaeology and Ethnology
www.sfu.ca/archaeology/museum/galltour/totemgal.htm

Glossary

adze: a tool that is similar to an ax

ancestors: family members that lived long ago

cultural symbol: something that represents the lifestyle of a group of people

fells: cuts down a tree

First Nations: Canada's original inhabitants

heritage: evidence of the past

mineral: a substance found in nature that is not an animal or plant

potlatch: special First Nations ceremony of sharing

tradition: something that has been done in a certain way for a long time

Index